— *The Ultimate* —
BAGEL
Cookbook

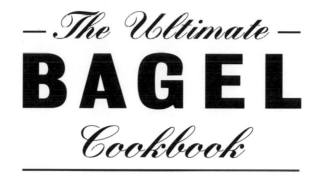

-The Ultimate-
BAGEL
Cookbook

BY
SARAH MAXWELL

CHARTWELL
BOOKS, INC.

A QUINTET BOOK

Published by Chartwell Books
A Division of Book Sales, Inc.
PO Box 7100
Edison, New Jersey 08818-7100

This edition produced for sale in the U.S.A., its
territories and dependencies only.

ISBN 0–7858–0245–2

This book was designed and produced by
Quintet Publishing Limited
6 Blundell Street
London N7 9BH

Creative Director: Richard Dewing
Designer: Isobel Gillan
Senior Editor: Laura Sandelson
Editor: Barbara Croxford
Photographer: Tim Hill
Home Economist and Stylist: Sarah Maxwell

Typeset in Great Britain by
Central Southern Typesetters, Eastbourne
Manufactured in Hong Kong by Regent Publishing Services Ltd.
Printed in China by Leefung-Asco Printers Ltd.

Author Acknowledgements
With special thanks to my grandma and poppa, Norma, Lok Zen and, as
always, Jenny, Paul and Oliver whose love, help and support make it all
worthwhile.

CONTENTS

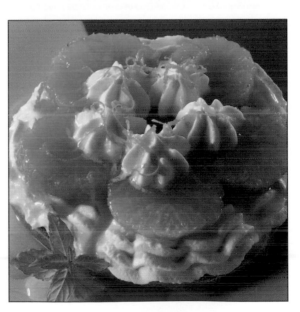

INTRODUCTION

★ ★ ★ ★ ★

You say Bagel, I say Beigel . . . basically depends on whether you are of Polish or Russian origin. At the end of the day, we all know we are talking about the one and only bread roll of its kind – unique in taste, texture, and method of cooking. Being the only type of bread that is boiled before it is baked, gives the bagel that distinguishable crispiness on the outside and delectable chewiness on the inside.

While bakers compete vigorously to create the most authentic bagel, the customer is in hot pursuit of the most scrumptious and original bagel filling. *The Bagel Book* is positively oozing with delicious fillings for bagels, ranging from the more classic to the very exotic, from the totally meatless to the sweet temptations in the last chapter.

Quantities are given to serve small numbers on the basis that bagels satisfy an instant craving, a spontaneous desire when there is only you and perhaps one other person around at the same time

with the same addiction. Other recipes cater for large numbers; but whatever the recipe, you only need to increase or reduce the quantities of ingredients to fill more or fewer bagels.

The essence of this book is light-hearted and fun, offering plenty of delicious ideas for bagel fillings. Choose your favorite bagel, such as sesame or poppy seed, onion or plain, to go with your favorite filling. Go crazy and experiment. These recipes can be used for ideas which you can adapt and change to suit your own personal tastes and desires.

STORING BAGELS
There is no doubt that bagels are best eaten fresh on the day they are made. However, day old bagels can be warmed in the oven or cut in half and toasted. They can also be frozen in airtight bags or containers for up to 3 months. These will need to be warmed in the oven from frozen, or toasted before filling and serving.

ABOVE Black Forest Bagel (see page 90)

LEFT Bagels are round, boiled rolls with a hole in the middle, symbolizing the continuous circle of life.

BASIC BAGELS

★ ★ ★

This recipe makes about sixteen bagels of average size. If you prefer your bagels slightly bigger or smaller than average, then you can make them to suit your preference. Bear in mind, the bigger they are the fewer bagels you will make and vice versa.

MAKES ABOUT 16 BAGELS

1 cup boiling milk

¼ cup butter, plus extra for greasing

2 tbsp caster sugar

1 tbsp fresh yeast or 2 tsp dried

pinch of salt

1 egg, separated

3½ cups all-purpose flour

2 tbsp milk

METHOD

Pour the boiling milk into a mixing bowl and stir in the butter and sugar. Leave the mixture to stand until lukewarm.

Sprinkle over the yeast and leave to stand in a warm place for about 5 minutes for fresh yeast and about 15 minutes for dried, until the mixture is frothy.

Stir the salt and egg white into the yeast mixture, then gradually beat in the flour to make a soft dough. Turn the dough onto a lightly floured surface and knead for about 5 minutes, until smooth and elastic.

Return the dough to the cleaned bowl and cover with plastic wrap. Leave in a warm place to rise for about 1 hour, or until doubled in size.

Turn the risen dough out onto the work surface and knock back to its original size. Divide the dough into sixteen even-sized pieces.

Roll a piece of dough into a "sausage" shape, then wrap it around your fingers on one hand to make a "hoop" shape. Pinch the join together firmly and repeat with the other pieces of dough.

Place the bagels on greased baking sheets covered with greased waxed paper. Leave enough space between them so they can rise without touching, then cover loosely with a piece of plastic wrap. Return the bagels to a warm place to rise for about 10 minutes.

Preheat the oven to 400°F. Bring a large saucepan of water to the boil, then reduce the heat and simmer. Gently drop the bagels into the water, only a few at a time to prevent them touching.

Simmer the bagels for about 15–20 seconds, or until puffy and beginning to swell. Using a slotted spoon, lift the bagels out of the water and return to the baking sheets. Repeat the process with the remaining bagels.

Mix together the egg yolk and milk in a small bowl. Lightly brush the bagels evenly with the egg glaze. Bake for about 20 minutes, or until risen, golden, and hollow sounding when tapped. Transfer to a wire rack to cool.

VARIATIONS

★ ★ ★

POPPY SEED BAGELS

Sprinkle the bagels generously with poppy seeds after they have been glazed.

SESAME SEED BAGELS

Sprinkle the bagels generously with sesame seeds after they have been glazed.

ONION BAGELS

Heat 3 tbsp vegetable oil in a large frying pan and add 2 large finely chopped onions. Cook for about 10 minutes or until golden brown. Drain. Place a little of the fried onion on the top of the bagels after they have been glazed.

CINNAMON AND RAISIN BAGELS

Substitute 1¼ cups of the all-purpose flour with wholewheat flour and add 1 cup raisins and 1 tbsp ground cinnamon to the dry ingredients. Stir well and continue following the recipe.

BAGEL CHIPS

★ ★ ★ ★ ★

*A perfect anytime snack made with day-old bagels. Use your
imagination when it comes to your own favorite flavorings, but
you'll have a hard time beating the great taste of this recipe.*

SERVES 4–6

2 onion bagels

sunflower oil, for shallow frying

2 cloves of garlic, crushed

pinch of dried mixed herbs

salt and freshly ground black pepper

3–4 tbsp freshly grated Parmesan cheese

METHOD

Cut the bagels into small, bite-size pieces.

Heat the oil in a frying pan and add the garlic and mixed herbs. Cook for about 1 minute. Add the bagel pieces in batches, turning them for about 3–5 minutes, or until golden brown and crisp.

Drain the bagel chips on absorbent paper towels. Serve in a warm serving dish, seasoned with salt and pepper and sprinkled with freshly grated Parmesan cheese.

CLASSIC BAGELS

★ ★ ★ ★ ★

SUNDAY BEST
★ ★ ★ ★ ★

Make use of the leftover roast in this delicious bagel filling.

SERVES 2

2 onion bagels

butter or margarine, for spreading

¼ lb chilled roast beef, thinly sliced

2 tomatoes, thinly sliced

3–4 tbsp horseradish sauce

salt and freshly ground black pepper

METHOD

Cut the bagels in half horizontally and lightly butter the cut surfaces.

Pile the roast beef onto the base of each bagel, then top with slices of fresh tomato.

Spread over a little horseradish. Season with salt and freshly ground black pepper, before putting on the lid.

TOWER OF BAGEL
★ ★ ★ ★ ★

Not one, but two delicious layers of smooth, soft creamy cheese topped with wafer thin slices of velvety smoked salmon.

SERVES 2

2 sesame bagels

butter or margarine, for spreading

½ cup cream cheese

3 oz smoked salmon, sliced wafer thin

tiny fresh dill sprigs

½ lemon, for squeezing

freshly ground black pepper

capers and sweet pickles, to serve

METHOD

Using a large serrated knife, slice the bagels into three layers. Butter the bottom layer and top surface of the middle layer sparingly.

Spread a generous layer of cream cheese on top of the buttered layers. Top with sliced smoked salmon, cutting and folding it to fit the bagel.

Scatter a few tiny sprigs of fresh dill over the smoked salmon and sprinkle with a squeeze of lemon juice. Grind some freshly ground black pepper over the top and layer up the bagel, finishing with the sesame coated lid. Serve with capers and sweet pickles.

Tower of Bagel

BROOKLYN BAGEL

★ ★ ★ ★ ★

*Corned beef is at its best when fresh, moist, warm, and crumbly.
Piled into a soft, chewy bagel with all the trimmings,
it's unbeatable!*

SERVES 2

2 poppy seed bagels

butter or margarine, for spreading

mild mustard

6 oz warm fresh corned beef, sliced

½ cup sliced cooked beet

2 small pickles

cocktail onions and fresh parsley sprigs, to garnish

METHOD

Cut the bagels in half horizontally and lightly butter the cut surfaces.

Spread a thin layer of mustard on the base of each bagel and pile the sliced corned beef on top. Add a little more mustard, if you like it hot, then add a layer of beet, then sliced pickles.

Place the bagel lids on top and serve with cocktail onions and parsley sprigs.

FRIDAY NIGHT BAGEL

★ ★ ★ ★ ★

Chopped liver is a Jewish delicacy, available from Jewish delicatessens and major supermarkets, and usually served at the Sabbath on Friday nights.

SERVES 2

2 plain or caraway bagels

butter or margarine, for spreading

3 oz chopped liver

1 hard-boiled egg

chopped fresh parsley, to garnish

lettuce leaves and sweet pickles, to serve

METHOD

Cut the bagels in half horizontally and lightly butter the cut surfaces.

Generously pile the chopped liver on the base of each bagel. Spread out evenly and make line indentations with the knife.

Separate the yolk from the white of the egg. Press separately through a sieve onto a small plate. Use the sieved white and yolk of the egg to fill the lines in the chopped liver, making lines across the surface.

Sprinkle with chopped parsley and top with the bagel lid. Serve with a little lettuce and sweet pickles.

THE BIG DIPPER

★ ★ ★ ★ ★

For dieting bagel-lovers everywhere, this one's for you. Piles of cool, fresh cottage cheese, served with a slice of juicy pineapple and topped with crisp cubes of cucumber.

SERVES 2

1 bagel

¼ cup cottage cheese

sprouts

2 slices of canned pineapple in fruit juice, drained

⅓ cup finely diced cucumber

salt and freshly ground black pepper

yellow pickled onions and fresh dill sprigs, to serve

METHOD

Cut the bagel in half horizontally and place each half on an individual plate.

Divide the cottage cheese between the bagel halves and spread out evenly. Arrange a layer of sprouts in a circle on top.

Place a slice of pineapple on top of the sprouts, then pile half the diced cucumber in the center of each. Season with salt and black pepper. Serve with yellow pickled onions and dill sprigs.

BENEDICT BAGEL

★ ★ ★ ★ ★

The combination of the melted cheese and soft poached egg dripping in the subtle taste of hollandaise sauce makes this melt-in-the-mouth bagel a perfect breakfast or lunchtime snack.

SERVES 2

2 bagels

¼ cup thinly sliced Cheddar cheese

2 eggs

a little butter or margarine

4 tbsp hollandaise sauce

chopped fresh parsley and parsley sprigs, to garnish

METHOD

Slice the tops off the bagels and toast the bases. Leave the bagels on the grill pan and top with the sliced cheese.

Poach the eggs in a little butter until they are cooked the way you like them.

Just before the end of the cooking time, broil the cheese topped bagels to melt the cheese. Place the bagel bases on individual serving plates and top each with a poached egg.

Drizzle on the hollandaise sauce and sprinkle over the chopped parsley. Replace the bagel lids. Garnish with the parsley sprigs and serve immediately.

DELI SPECIAL BAGEL

★ ★ ★ ★ ★

Some like it hot! Packed full of succulent salamis and peppery pickles, this bagel will certainly liven up your palate!

SERVES 2

2 poppy seed bagels

butter or margarine, for spreading

2 tbsp relish

2 oz pastrami

1 oz beef salami

mild mustard

pickled chilies, to serve

METHOD

Cut the bagels horizontally into three even layers and lightly spread with butter.

Spread the relish over the bottom layers. Pile the pastrami on top of the relish, then put on the middle bagel layers.

Arrange the beef salami on top and add enough mustard to suit your taste. Put the bagel lids on and serve with pickled chilies.

Deli Special Bagel

BROADWAY BAGEL

★ ★ ★ ★ ★

A classic breakfast bagel – filled with hash browns and a fried egg!

SERVES 2

1 small onion, finely chopped

1 large potato, peeled and grated

pinch of dried thyme

salt and freshly ground black pepper

¼ cup butter or margarine, plus extra for spreading

2 eggs

2 bagels

METHOD

In a mixing bowl, combine the onion, potato, dried thyme, and salt and black pepper. Mix well.

Melt a little more than half of the butter in a large non-stick frying pan and add the potato mixture. Flatten it out in the pan and cook for about 10 minutes.

Turn the hash browns over, don't worry if they break up, and continue to cook for about 5–10 minutes until golden. Just before the end of the cooking time, melt the remaining butter in another frying pan and fry the eggs, turning them over, if you like.

Cut the bagels in half horizontally and toast. Lightly butter the cut surfaces, then put the bases on individual plates.

Pile on the hash browns, then put an egg on top. Season again with salt and freshly ground black pepper, then serve with the bagel lids.

ITALIAN BAGEL

★ ★ ★ ★ ★

This is a mouth-watering combination of some of the finest Italian ingredients.
Where better to combine them than inside a warm, fresh bagel?

SERVES 2

2 sesame seed bagels

a little extra virgin olive oil

¼ cup very thinly sliced Milano salami

½ cup sliced mozzarella cheese

2 tomatoes, sliced

fresh basil leaves, torn

salt and freshly ground black pepper

mayonnaise, to taste

black and green Italian olives, to serve

METHOD

Cut the bagels in half horizontally and lightly brush the cut surfaces with a little olive oil.

Arrange the salami on the base of each bagel, then place a layer of Mozzarella cheese on top.

Divide the tomato slices and the torn basil leaves between the bagels, then season with salt and freshly ground black pepper.

Spoon over some mayonnaise, then top with the bagel lids. Cut in half and serve with Italian olives.

HERRING LOVER'S BAGEL

★ ★ ★ ★ ★

*If you like herring, then this creamy herring topped bagel
is for you.*

SERVES 2

1 bagel

butter or margarine, for spreading

4 oz jar skinned pickled herring fillets with onion

3 tbsp light cream

freshly ground black pepper

1 tbsp chopped fresh dill

lemon wedges and fresh dill sprigs, to garnish

METHOD

Cut the bagel in half horizontally and toast on both sides. Lightly butter the cut surfaces.

In a small bowl combine the herring, cream, freshly ground black pepper, and chopped dill. Stir to coat the fish in the sauce.

Pile the herring mixture onto the bagel halves. Serve garnished with lemon wedges and fresh dill sprigs.

HOT TUNA BAGEL

★ ★ ★ ★ ★

A delicious combination of tender pieces of tuna and crunchy bell peppers.

SERVES 2

2 sesame seed bagels

butter or margarine, for spreading

few leaves of lettuce, washed

7 oz can tuna chunks in vegetable oil, drained

½ orange pepper, seeded and finely diced

½ green bell pepper, seeded and finely diced

1 small onion, very finely chopped

3–4 tbsp mayonnaise, plus extra for drizzling

juice of ½ lemon

salt and freshly ground black pepper

½ tsp chili powder

½ tsp ground turmeric

fresh dill sprigs, to garnish

METHOD

Cut the bagels in half horizontally and lightly spread the cut surfaces with butter. Place the top halves upside down on serving plates and arrange a few of the lettuce leaves on top.

In a mixing bowl, combine the tuna, diced bell peppers, onion, mayonnaise, and lemon juice and season with salt and black pepper. Stir gently to mix.

Divide the tuna mixture between the bagels, reserving about two tablespoons in the bowl. Top with the other half of each bagel. Shred the remaining lettuce and arrange on top of each bagel. Spoon over the remaining tuna mixture and drizzle over extra mayonnaise.

Sprinkle over the chili powder and ground turmeric. Garnish each with a sprig of fresh dill.

CLUB CLASS BAGEL

★ ★ ★ ★ ★

A first class bagel, made with only the finest ingredients.

SERVES 2

2 poppy seed bagels

butter or margarine, for spreading

a few lettuce leaves, washed

3 oz wafer thin pastrami

1 tomato, thinly sliced

3 oz wafer thin chicken or turkey breast

2 tbsp mild or hot mustard

salt and freshly ground black pepper

METHOD

Cut the bagels horizontally into three even layers and lightly butter. Tear the lettuce leaves into pieces and arrange on the bottom layer of each bagel.

Pile the pastrami on top of the lettuce, then position the middle layer of bagel. Arrange the tomato slices, then a single layer of wafer thin chicken or turkey on top.

Spoon over the mustard, then add the remaining chicken or turkey. Season with salt and freshly ground black pepper. Place the bagel lids on top and serve.

BAGEL-BURGER
★ ★ ★ ★ ★

This double burger bagel is a complete meal in itself. Forget the fries, who needs them?

SERVES 2

2 sesame seed bagels

4 × ¼ lb burgers

few crisp lettuce leaves, washed

1 tomato, thinly sliced

2 slices Cheddar cheese

4 tbsp ketchup

2 tbsp mayonnaise

fresh parsley sprigs, to garnish

METHOD
Cut the bagels in half horizontally and set aside. Fry the burgers until cooked to your taste. Place a few lettuce leaves on the base of each bagel and top with tomato slices.

About a minute before the burgers are cooked, place a slice of cheese on top of two of them and cook until just melting. Place the cheese topped burgers on top of the tomato layer of each bagel and top with a little ketchup.

Position the other burger on top and add a little more ketchup with some mayonnaise. Put on the bagel lid and serve on a few lettuce leaves, garnished with fresh parsley sprigs.

DOUBLE CHEESE MELT
★ ★ ★ ★ ★

This is no ordinary cheese sandwich! The layers of delicately flavored cheese, salad, and dressing create a bagel to savor as it melts in your mouth.

SERVES 2

2 bagels

butter or margarine, for spreading

¾ cup grated Swiss cheese

¾ cup grated Cheddar cheese

2 tbsp mayonnaise

2 tsp French dressing

salt and freshly ground black pepper

1 tomato, sliced

few leaves of crisp lettuce, shredded

pickles, to serve

METHOD
Cut the bagels horizontally into three even layers and lightly butter them.

Divide the Swiss cheese between the two bottom layers and the Cheddar cheese between the two middle layers. Lightly broil the cheese layers, until just melting.

In a small bowl mix together the mayonnaise and French dressing and season with salt and freshly ground black pepper.

Arrange the sliced tomato on top of the Swiss cheese and drizzle over a little of the dressing mixture. Place the Cheddar layer on top.

Divide the lettuce between the bagels and drizzle over a little more dressing. Put the bagel lids on and serve immediately with a few pickles.

Bagel-Burger

GRANDMA'S SPECIAL

★ ★ ★ ★ ★

A classic in any traditional Jewish household – just like Grandma used to make.

SERVES 2

3 hard-boiled eggs, shelled and chopped

6 tbsp chopped green onion tops

4 tbsp mayonnaise

salt and freshly ground black pepper

2 sesame seed bagels

butter or margarine, for spreading

1 tbsp chopped fresh parsley

pickles, to serve

METHOD

First make the egg mayonnaise. Place the chopped egg, green onion tops, mayonnaise, and salt and freshly ground black pepper in a bowl and mix until evenly combined.

Cut the bagels in half horizontally and butter the cut surfaces. Divide the egg mayonnaise between the base of each bagel and sprinkle over the chopped parsley. Top with the bagel lids.

Serve cut in half crosswise with pickles.

SWISS CHEESE BAGEL

★ ★ ★ ★ ★

You will savor every bite of this freshly baked onion bagel, packed
full of wafer thin slices of subtle tasting Swiss cheese.

SERVES 2

2 onion bagels

butter or margarine, for spreading

½ ripe avocado, sliced

few drops of freshly squeezed lemon juice

¾ cup thinly sliced Swiss cheese

salt and freshly ground black pepper

fresh parsley sprigs, to garnish

METHOD

Cut the bagels in half horizontally and lightly butter the cut surfaces.

Divide the sliced avocado between the bases of the bagels and sprinkle over a few drops of lemon juice.

Pile the Swiss cheese on top of the avocado and season with salt and freshly ground black pepper. Put on the bagel lids and garnish with sprigs of fresh parsley.

BIG BANG BAGEL

★ ★ ★ ★ ★

One of the more complicated fillings, but well worth the effort.

SERVES 2

2 tbsp olive oil

1 small onion, finely chopped

1 clove of garlic, crushed

1 lb ground beef

2 tbsp tomato paste

7 oz can red kidney beans, drained

1 cup stock

1 tbsp flour

1–2 tbsp chili powder

pinch of dried oregano

salt and freshly ground black pepper

2 bagels

4 tbsp sour cream

2 tbsp snipped fresh chives

METHOD

First make the chili. Heat the oil in a saucepan and add the onion and garlic. Cook for about 5 minutes, then stir in the ground beef. Cook, stirring frequently, for about 10 minutes, then add the tomato paste, kidney beans, and stock.

Mix the flour and chili powder together in a small bowl with a little water to make a smooth paste. Stir into the meat mixture with the oregano and season with salt and freshly ground black pepper. Simmer the chilli for about 1 hour, stirring occasionally.

Cut the bagels in half horizontally and place each half on a separate serving plate. Spoon the chili on top of the bagel halves and top with sour cream and chives. Serve immediately.

PINK CADILLAC

★ ★ ★ ★ ★

An interesting layered bagel filled with salmon, salad, and mayonnaise.

SERVES 2

1 large sesame seed bagel

butter or margarine, for spreading

¾ cup grated cucumber

7 oz can pink salmon in vegetable oil, drained

¼ red pepper, seeded and very finely diced

2–3 tbsp mayonnaise

squeeze of fresh lemon juice

salt and freshly ground black pepper

fresh dill sprigs, lemon and lime slices, to garnish

METHOD

Thinly cut the bagel horizontally into five even slices and lightly butter.

Lay the bagel slices out on a work surface. Except for the lid, divide the grated cucumber between the layers.

To make the salmon filling, place the salmon in a bowl and add the diced pepper, mayonnaise, lemon juice, and salt and freshly ground black pepper. Stir to mix.

Divide the salmon mixture between the bagel slices, then sprinkle a few tiny dill sprigs over each layer. Pile up on a serving plate, finishing with the lid. Serve garnished with fresh dill sprigs and lemon and lime slices.

Pink Cadillac

BAGEL PARMESAN

★ ★ ★ ★ ★

A definite Mediterranean-style bagel — warm and garlicky. This one makes a delicious appetizer or snack.

SERVES 4

2 bagels

2 cloves of garlic, quartered

¼ cup extra virgin olive oil

14 oz can artichoke hearts, drained and quartered

4 oz jar antipasto with carrots and olives in oil, drained

3–4 tbsp chopped green onion tops

1 cup freshly grated Parmesan cheese

freshly ground black pepper

fresh parsley sprigs, to garnish

METHOD

Cut the bagels in half horizontally and toast the cut surfaces. Put the garlic in a small cup and add the olive oil. Stir and set aside.

Arrange the artichoke pieces on the toasted bagel halves and scatter over some of the antipasto and the green onion tops. Sprinkle over the Parmesan cheese and ground black pepper, then generously drizzle over the garlic oil.

Broil the bagels for 2–3 minutes, just to melt the cheese slightly. Serve immediately on individual serving plates, garnished with the reserved antipasto and sprigs of fresh parsley.

CALIFORNIA DREAM

★ ★ ★ ★ ★

*Healthy, crisp, and crunchy, this bagel makes the perfect
light lunch snack.*

SERVES 2

2 plain bagels

butter or margarine, for spreading

1 red apple, cored and chopped

1 stick of celery, sliced

¼ cup raisins

¼ cup shelled peanuts

2–3 tbsp mayonnaise

salt and freshly ground black pepper

1 tbsp chopped parsley

parsley sprig, to garnish

METHOD

Cut the bagels in half horizontally and lightly butter
the surfaces. Cut the top halves into quarters.

To make the filling: in a mixing bowl, combine the
apple, celery, raisins, peanuts, mayonnaise, and salt
and freshly ground black pepper. Stir well to mix.

Pile the apple mixture onto the base of each bagel
and place on individual serving plates. Arrange the
bagel quarters around the bases and serve each one
garnished with a sprig of parsley.

THE LONE RANGER
★ ★ ★ ★ ★

A good camp fire bagel or a perfect one for the children's supper.

SERVES 4

4 sausages

2 onion bagels

butter or margarine, for spreading

14 oz can baked beans

1 cup grated Cheddar cheese

METHOD
Grill the sausages for about 10 minutes, turning frequently, until cooked through.

Cut the bagels in half horizontally and toast. Lightly butter the cut surfaces, then place on individual serving plates.

Heat the baked beans in a saucepan. When the sausages are cooked, spoon the baked beans onto the bagel halves and place a sausage on top. Sprinkle over the grated cheese and serve.

GRAND SLAM BAGEL
★ ★ ★ ★ ★

Dripping with juicy meaty flavors, the fried mushrooms and melted cheese make this a bagel to remember.

SERVES 2

2 poppy seed bagels

2 minute steaks

3 cups baby button mushrooms, washed

2–4 tbsp mild mustard

2–4 tbsp ketchup

salt and freshly ground black pepper

1 cup grated sharp Cheddar cheese

fresh thyme sprigs, to garnish

METHOD
Cut the bagels in half horizontally and toast. Cut each round in half, to make four crescent shapes.

Heat a non-stick frying pan and fry the steaks with the mushrooms for about 5 minutes, or until the mushrooms have browned and the steak is cooked to your liking. Turn the steaks over halfway through cooking.

Arrange the bottom bagel crescents in an "s" shape on individual serving plates and spread with mustard.

Place a steak on top and then scatter over the mushrooms. Top with ketchup, season with salt and freshly ground black pepper, then position the bagel lids on top.

Sprinkle over the grated cheese. Broil the bagels for a few minutes, until the cheese has melted. Serve immediately, garnished with sprigs of fresh thyme.

Grand Slam Bagel

EXOTIC
BAGELS

★ ★ ★ ★ ★

TEX MEX BAGEL

★ ★ ★ ★ ★

This chili-hot filling of tuna, corn, and kidney beans is perfectly complemented by the tangy lemon dressing to cool you down.

SERVES 2

7 oz can tuna chunks in water, drained

⅓ cup drained canned corn

⅓ cup drained canned red kidney beans

pinch of chili powder

1 bagel

butter or margarine, for spreading

fresh chilies, to garnish

For the dressing

2 tbsp olive oil

1 clove of garlic, crushed

1 tbsp white wine vinegar

1 tsp freshly squeezed lemon juice

1 tbsp mayonnaise

salt and freshly ground black pepper

METHOD

To make the filling, place the tuna, corn, and kidney beans in a bowl and combine with the chili powder. Set aside.

To make the dressing, place all the ingredients in a cup or blender and mix until evenly blended.

Cut the bagel in half horizontally and toast. Lightly butter the cut surfaces and place the bagel halves on individual serving plates.

Spoon the tuna filling on top of each bagel half, then drizzle over the dressing. Serve immediately, garnished with fresh chilies.

PESTO PIZZA BAGEL

★ ★ ★ ★ ★

*A mouth-watering taste of the Mediterranean with plenty of basil
and oregano, this pizza is laced with melted Mozzarella cheese.*

SERVES 2

1 sesame seed bagel

4–5 tbsp extra virgin olive oil

2 cloves of garlic, quartered

2–3 tsp tomato paste

¼ cup pitted black olives

2 tomatoes, chopped

1 tbsp pesto sauce

½ cup grated Mozzarella cheese

pinch of dried oregano

salt and freshly ground black pepper

fresh herbs, to garnish

METHOD

Cut the bagel in half horizontally and toast. In a small cup, combine the olive oil and garlic. Stir and leave to stand for about 15 minutes.

Drizzle a little garlic oil over the bagel halves and set aside on a baking sheet.

In a bowl, combine the tomato paste, olives, and tomatoes with the pesto sauce. Stir well, then pile onto the bagel halves.

Scatter over the grated Mozzarella cheese, drizzle with remaining garlic oil, discarding the cloves. Sprinkle with oregano and season with salt and freshly ground black pepper.

Bake the pizza bagels in a preheated oven at 400°F for about 5–10 minutes, or until the cheese has melted and the bagel bases are crisp. Serve immediately, garnished with fresh herbs.

MILLION DOLLAR BAGEL

★ ★ ★ ★ ★

An elite bagel for a very special occasion.

SERVES 2

1 bagel

butter or margarine, for spreading

2–3 tbsp black caviar

1 tsp sour cream

1 hard-boiled egg, shelled and sliced

fresh dill sprigs, to garnish

METHOD

Cut the bagel in half horizontally and lightly butter the cut surfaces.

Spread each bagel half generously with the caviar and level the surface. Use a teaspoon to drizzle over the sour cream in a spiral pattern.

Serve with hard-boiled egg slices, garnished with sprigs of dill.

FESTIVE FILLER

★ ★ ★ ★ ★

Full of the festive spirit, this bagel combines blue cheese, walnuts, and grapes. Serve with a glass of port for the perfect snack over the festive season.

SERVES 2

1 bagel

butter or margarine, for spreading

1 cup crumbled blue cheese

½ cup chopped walnuts

½ cup peeled and chopped seedless green grapes

1–2 tbsp blue cheese dressing

2 tbsp chopped fresh parsley

salt and freshly ground black pepper

METHOD

Cut the bagel in half horizontally and butter the cut surfaces.

Combine the blue cheese, walnuts, and grapes in a bowl. Stir in the blue cheese dressing.

Pile the cheese mixture onto the bagel halves and sprinkle over the chopped parsley. Season with salt and freshly ground black pepper and serve.

Million Dollar Bagel

BOMBAY BAGEL

★ ★ ★ ★ ★

The delicious combination of tomato and egg, draped in a mild and creamy curried sauce, is dusted with a sprinkling of fresh coriander.

SERVES 2

1 bagel

butter or margarine, for spreading

2 hard-boiled eggs, shelled and cut into small pieces

1 cup quartered cherry tomatoes

1 tbsp mild curry paste

3–4 tbsp mayonnaise

1 tbsp milk

2 tbsp chopped fresh coriander

fresh coriander sprigs, to garnish

METHOD

Cut the bagel in half horizontally and lightly butter the cut surfaces. Cut each half into two equal shapes.

Arrange the pieces of egg and tomato on the bagel quarters. Mix the curry paste and mayonnaise together in a small bowl, then stir in the milk.

Drizzle the sauce evenly over the bagels and serve immediately, sprinkled with chopped fresh coriander and garnished with a few coriander sprigs.

EL BAGEL

★ ★ ★ ★ ★

*A simple yet extremely effective party piece, which can be
prepared from the cupboard in minutes. Guests will definitely be impressed.*

SERVES 3—4

1 bagel

6 oz jar pimiento in tomato sauce

olive oil, to drizzle

parsley sprig

METHOD

Cut the bagel in half horizontally and toast. Cut each
half into quarter pieces.

Top each bagel piece with a teaspoon of pimiento
sauce and arrange on a serving plate.

Drizzle with a little olive oil and serve garnished
with a sprig of parsley.

BANGKOK BAGEL

★ ★ ★ ★ ★

A Thai salad of tender pieces of chicken, wafer thin slices of carrot,
and shredded lettuce, coated in a warm peanut sauce.

SERVES 2

2 sesame seed bagels

1 cooked chicken breast fillet, skinned and sliced into thin strips

1 small carrot, peeled

½ crisp lettuce heart, shredded

3–4 tbsp peanut sauce (satay sauce) from a jar

freshly ground black pepper

lemon grass, fresh chilies, and coriander, to garnish

METHOD

Cut the bagels in half horizontally and set aside.
    Place the chicken strips in a bowl. Using a vegetable peeler, slice wafer thin strips from the carrot and add to the bowl with the shredded lettuce.
    Warm the peanut sauce in a small saucepan, then add to the bowl. Stir gently to coat the ingredients.
    Pile the salad onto the bagel halves, then season with freshly ground black pepper. Serve garnished with lemon grass, fresh chilies, and coriander.

GREENPEACE

★ ★ ★ ★ ★

The creamy, smooth texture of ripe avocado makes this pale green
topping a delicious dinner party dish.

SERVES 4

2 bagels

butter or margarine, for spreading

1 ripe avocado, peeled

freshly squeezed juice of ½ lemon

3–4 tbsp sour cream

1 tbsp snipped fresh chives

salt and freshly ground black pepper

fresh chives, to garnish

METHOD

Cut the bagels in half horizontally, then cut each half into a crescent. Butter the cut surfaces and set aside.
    Place the avocado in a mixing bowl with the lemon juice, sour cream, snipped chives, and salt and freshly ground black pepper. Mash the mixture with a fork or potato masher, until smooth.
    Pile the avocado mixture onto the bagel pieces and arrange on a serving plate. Serve garnished with fresh chives.

Bangkok Bagel

BARBECUE BAGEL

★ ★ ★ ★ ★

Make up your own kebobs using your favorite ingredients. Fish kebobs, using chunks of fish, are extremely good.

SERVES 2

4 button mushrooms

¼ red pepper, seeded and cut into pieces

¼ yellow pepper, seeded and cut into pieces

1 large chicken breast fillet, skinned and cut into thin strips

4 cherry tomatoes

1 bagel

butter or margarine, for spreading

few lettuce leaves, to serve

For the marinade

4 tbsp olive oil

1 tbsp white wine vinegar

1 tsp wholegrain mustard

1 tsp freshly squeezed lemon juice

salt and freshly ground black pepper

METHOD

To make the kebobs, thread the mushrooms, pepper pieces, chicken, and tomatoes onto four small wooden skewers. Lay the kebobs on a baking sheet.

To make the marinade, combine all the ingredients in a small bowl and whisk until evenly blended. Pour the marinade over the kebabs and leave for about 15 minutes at room temperature.

Cover the ends of the wooden skewers with small pieces of foil to prevent burning. Grill the kebobs for about 10 minutes, turning frequently in the marinade during cooking, until the chicken is cooked through.

Just before the end of the cooking time, cut the bagel in half horizontally and toast the cut surfaces. Lightly butter and arrange a little lettuce on top. Serve each bagel half with two kebobs, drizzling over any remaining marinade.

FALAFEBAGEL

★ ★ ★ ★ ★

*Falafel are a Middle Eastern speciality made from ground gazbanzo beans
and spices. Good package mixes are available from most supermarkets
and delicatessens, just follow the manufacturers' instructions.*

SERVES 2

16 small falafel balls, made according to the package
instructions

sunflower oil, for deep frying

1 poppy seed bagel

3–4 tbsp hummus

1 tomato, sliced

¼ cup finely diced cucumber

3–4 tbsp tahini sauce

1 tbsp chopped fresh mint

fresh mint sprigs, to garnish

METHOD

Deep-fry the falafel balls until crisp and golden. Drain
on absorbent paper towels.

Cut the bagel in half horizontally and put each half
on an individual serving plate. Spread the hummus
over each half, then top with the tomato slices.

Place the diced cucumber on top and divide the
falafel balls between them. Drizzle each bagel half
with tahini sauce and sprinkle over the chopped mint.
Garnish with sprigs of fresh mint.

BIARRITZ BAGEL

★ ★ ★ ★ ★

Where fresh sardines are plump and plentiful – this bagel uses the convenience variety with all the delicious flavors to remind you of sunny climes.

SERVES 2

1 sesame seed bagel

2 tsp tomato paste

3 oz can sardines in oil, drained

1 small tomato, chopped

salt and freshly ground black pepper

pinch of chopped fresh parsley

lemon wedges and parsley sprigs, to garnish

METHOD

Cut the bagel in half horizontally and toast the cut surfaces. Spread the tomato paste over each bagel half.

Turn the sardines into a bowl and roughly mash with a fork. Stir in the chopped tomato and season with salt and freshly ground black pepper.

Pile the sardine mixture onto each bagel half, then broil for about 5 minutes. Serve sprinkled with chopped parsley and garnished with lemon wedges and parsley sprigs.

BEIJING BAGEL

★ ★ ★ ★ ★

*With a taste of the Orient, this bagel is topped with a delicately
flavored combination of stir-fried chicken and vegetables.*

SERVES 2

1 tbsp sesame oil

1 clove of garlic, crushed

1 tsp finely grated fresh ginger

½ orange pepper, seeded and thinly sliced

1 cooked chicken breast fillet, skinned and cut into thin strips

½ cup baby corn, cut in half lengthways

3–4 green onions, cut into thin strips

1 small carrot, finely shredded

¼ cup beansprouts

4–5 tbsp soy sauce

2 bagels

1 tsp sesame seeds

green onion tassels and parsley sprigs, to garnish

METHOD

To make the stir-fry, heat the sesame oil in a wok or
frying pan and stir-fry the garlic and ginger for about
1 minute.

Add the strips of pepper, then the chicken and
corn. Stir-fry for about 2–3 minutes, then add the
green onions, carrot, and finally the beansprouts. Stir
and cook for about 1 minute, then sprinkle with the
soy sauce and toss into the ingredients.

Cut the bagels in half horizontally and toast the cut
surfaces. Arrange two halves on each serving plate.

Pile the stir-fry onto the bagels, then sprinkle with
sesame seeds. Garnish with green onion tassels and
sprigs of parsley.

BEVERLY HILLS BAGEL

★ ★ ★ ★ ★

Melba toast bagels are wonderful served with this creamy smoked salmon paté.

SERVES 2

5 oz smoked salmon trimmings

2–3 tbsp heavy cream

2 tsp chopped fresh dill

few drops of freshly squeezed lemon juice

salt and freshly ground black pepper

2 bagels

butter curls and fresh dill sprigs, to garnish

METHOD

To make the paté, place the smoked salmon, cream, chopped dill, lemon juice, and salt and ground black pepper in a blender or food processor. Puree until smooth.

Cut the bagels in half horizontally. Slice the top half of each bagel into very thin slices, then toast everything, including the bases, on both sides.

Divide the paté between the bagel bases and serve on individual plates with the 'Melba toast' tops, butter curls, and sprigs of fresh dill.

RED ALERT
★ ★ ★ ★ ★

Hot and spicy, this red topping is delicious served on a toasted sesame seed bagel.

SERVES 2

15 ml/1 tbsp olive oil

½ red onion, chopped

1 clove of garlic, crushed

½ red pepper, seeded and diced

1 tbsp tomato paste

7 oz can chopped tomatoes, drained

pinch of cayenne pepper

1 tsp cumin seeds

1 tsp mustard seeds

salt and freshly ground black pepper

1 bagel

butter or margarine, for spreading

2–3 tbsp chopped fresh parsley

METHOD

Heat the oil in a frying pan and add the onion, garlic, and red pepper. Cook for about 5 minutes, until softened.

Stir in the tomato paste, tomatoes, and spices and season with salt and freshly ground black pepper. Cook gently for about 10 minutes, stirring frequently. Allow the mixture to cool.

Meanwhile, cut the bagel in half horizontally and toast. Butter, then top with the red mixture. Serve sprinkled with chopped fresh parsley.

VIENNESE BAGEL
★ ★ ★ ★ ★

A Vienna bagel hot dog with all the trimmings.

SERVES 2

2 Vienna sausages

1 tbsp sunflower oil

1 onion, sliced into thin rings

1 bagel

butter or margarine, for spreading

2–3 tbsp mild mustard

2–3 tbsp ketchup

salt and freshly ground black pepper

pickles, to serve

METHOD

Place the sausages in boiling water for about 5 minutes, or until heated through. Drain.

Meanwhile, heat the oil in a frying pan and fry the onion rings for about 5 minutes, until slightly golden.

Cut the bagel in half vertically then slice each crescent horizontally, almost right through. Lightly butter the cut surfaces.

To assemble the bagel halves place them, cut side up, on an individual serving plate. Place a sausage in the middle of each bagel half to resemble a hot dog roll.

Scatter a few fried onions on top of the sausages, then add the mustard and ketchup. Season with salt and freshly ground black pepper. Serve with pickles.

Viennese Bagel

FILET DE BAGEL

★ ★ ★ ★ ★

A fillet steak bagel fit for a dinner party. Serve with tender sweet carrots and sauteed potatoes.

SERVES 4

¼ cup butter or margarine

½ lb button mushrooms, sliced

4 small fillet steaks

1–2 tsp dried thyme

salt and freshly ground black pepper

2 sesame seed bagels

4 tbsp Bearnaise sauce

fresh thyme sprigs, to garnish

METHOD

Melt the butter or margarine in a large frying pan and saute the mushrooms for about 5 minutes.

Move the mushrooms to the side of the pan and add the steaks. Sprinkle over the thyme and season with salt and freshly ground black pepper. Cook for 5–10 minutes, depending on how rare you like your meat, turning the steaks over halfway through cooking.

Meanwhile, cut the bagels in half horizontally and toast the cut surfaces. Using a pastry brush, spread some of the cooking juices from the frying pan over the cut surfaces of the bagels.

Warm the Bearnaise sauce in a small saucepan. To serve the bagels, place the halves on individual serving plates, top with mushrooms, then a piece of steak.

Drizzle over the Bearnaise sauce and season with a little extra ground black pepper. Garnish with sprigs of fresh thyme.

POSH NOSH BAGEL

★ ★ ★ ★ ★

*This warm goats' cheese salad with a special dressing is served on
a lightly toasted bagel. It makes an excellent appetizer for a dinner party.*

SERVES 4

2 bagels

butter or margarine, for spreading

4 × 1 in slices of goats' cheese

few mixed salad leaves

parsley sprigs, to garnish

For the dressing

2 tbsp hazelnut oil

4 tbsp sunflower oil

2–3 tbsp white wine vinegar

1 tsp hot mustard

salt and freshly ground black pepper

METHOD

To make the dressing, combine all the ingredients in a small bowl and whisk until evenly blended. Set aside.

Cut the bagels in half horizontally and lightly toast the cut surfaces, then butter them.

Arrange the goats' cheese slices on a sheet of foil on a baking sheet. Broil for about 2–3 minutes, or until just melting and golden.

Place one cheese on each bagel half and place on individual serving plates with a few salad leaves. Pour over the dressing and serve immediately, garnished with sprigs of parsley.

GUACABAGEL

★ ★ ★ ★ ★

*An inventive way of serving bagels – the hollowed center enables
the flavors of the guacamole filling to seep into the walls of the
bagel and taste really scrumptious.*

SERVES 2

1 avocado, peeled

½ small onion, finely chopped

1 small clove of garlic, crushed

1 tomato, chopped

squeeze of fresh lemon juice

salt and freshly ground black pepper

pinch of chili powder

2 poppy seed bagels

paprika, for dusting

parsley and chilies, to garnish

METHOD

To make the guacamole, put the avocado, onion, garlic, tomato, lemon juice, salt and freshly ground black pepper, and chili powder in a blender or food processor. Puree until smooth.

Using a small, sharp knife, cut about ¼–½in down into the top of each bagel, very close to the outside edge. Cut all around the bagel. Repeat the process around the inside edge.

Cut out the inside section, to make a hollow, running around the bagel. Fill the bagel with the guacamole. Serve sprinkled with paprika. Garnish with sprigs of parsley and chilies.

PALM BEACH BAGEL

★ ★ ★ ★ ★

*Light and refreshing, this exotic salad of chicken, pineapple, and
coconut is complemented by the cool taste of fresh mint.*

SERVES 2

2 sesame seed bagels

2 tbsp mayonnaise

1 cooked chicken breast fillet, skinned and diced

3 oz canned pineapple, drained and thinly sliced

1 oz flaked coconut, toasted

fresh mint sprigs, to garnish

For the dressing

3 tbsp hazelnut oil

1 tbsp white wine vinegar

salt and freshly ground black pepper

2 tbsp chopped fresh mint

METHOD

Cut around the inside of each bagel, slightly in from
the edge. Scoop out the middle section of dough to
make a hollow.

Line the inside of the bagels with the mayonnaise,
spreading it evenly with the back of a teaspoon.

Combine the chicken, pineapple, and coconut in a
bowl. Mix together the dressing ingredients and pour
over the chicken mixture.

Toss the filling to coat in the dressing, then pile into
the bagels. Garnish with sprigs of fresh mint.

EGGPLANT BAGEL

★ ★ ★ ★ ★

*This creamy eggplant topping is perfect served on warm fresh
bagels for lunch or as an appetizer.*

SERVES 2—4

1 bagel

2 tbsp olive oil

2 cloves of garlic, crushed

1 small onion, finely chopped

1 small eggplant, cut into small pieces

½ cup heavy cream

salt and freshly ground black pepper

1–2 tbsp chopped fresh parsley

tomato wedges and fresh parsley sprigs, to garnish

METHOD

Cut the bagel in half horizontally, then cut each half
vertically into crescents.

Heat the oil in a frying pan and add the garlic and
onion. Saute for about 5 minutes, until the onion has
softened. Add the eggplant pieces and cook for about
5–7 minutes, until the eggplant is cooked and
browned.

Stir in the cream and season with salt and freshly
ground black pepper. Simmer for about 5 minutes,
then cool slightly.

Serve the eggplant mixture spooned onto the bagel
crescents. Sprinkle over the chopped parsley and
serve with tomato wedges and sprigs of parsley, to
garnish.

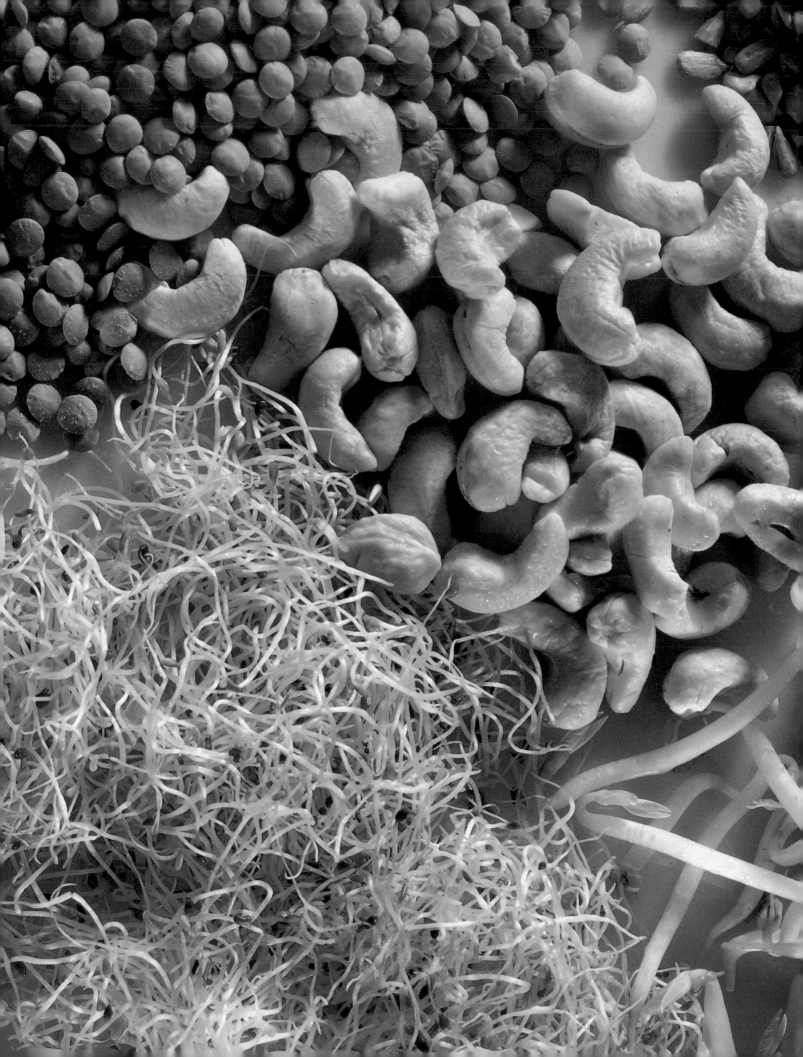

VEGETARIAN
BAGELS

★ ★ ★ ★ ★

MEDITERRANEAN BAGEL

★ ★ ★ ★ ★

Full of the flavors of the sun, this pepper, eggplant, and tomato filling is lightly cooked in virgin olive oil and garlic.

SERVES 2

3 tbsp extra virgin olive oil

2 cloves of garlic, crushed

½ red bell pepper, seeded and chopped

½ yellow bell pepper, seeded and chopped

½ small eggplant, cut into small pieces

¼ cup chopped sun dried tomatoes

2 tbsp tomato paste

2 tbsp dry red wine

salt and freshly ground black pepper

1 poppy seed bagel

2–3 tbsp chopped fresh parsley and basil

¼ cup freshly grated Parmesan cheese

fresh basil leaves, to garnish

METHOD

Heat the oil in a large frying pan and add the garlic, bell peppers, and eggplant. Cook for about 5 minutes, or until softened and lightly browned.

Add the sun dried tomatoes, tomato paste, red wine, and season with salt and freshly ground black pepper. Cook for another 5 minutes, stirring frequently. Cool slightly.

Meanwhile, cut the bagel in half horizontally and toast. Top each bagel half with the eggplant mixture and sprinkle with chopped fresh herbs. Scatter over the Parmesan cheese and serve garnished with fresh basil leaves.

TAVERNA BAGEL

★ ★ ★ ★ ★

A traditional combination of Greek salad ingredients, coated in an olive oil and lemon dressing.

SERVES 2

1 bagel

butter or margarine, for spreading

¾ cup cubed feta cheese

⅓ cup cubed cucumber

1 tomato, cut into pieces

½ cup pitted black olives

chopped fresh mint, finely grated lemon zest, fresh mint sprigs
and salad leaves, to garnish

For the dressing

1 clove of garlic, crushed

3 tbsp extra virgin olive oil

1–2 tbsp white wine vinegar

1 tsp freshly squeezed lemon juice

salt and freshly ground black pepper

METHOD

Cut the bagel in half horizontally and butter the cut
surfaces. Combine the feta cheese, cucumber,
tomato, and olives in a mixing bowl.

To make the dressing, place the garlic, oil, vinegar,
lemon juice, and salt and freshly ground black pepper
in a mixing bowl. Whisk, then pour over the salad
ingredients.

Divide the salad mixture between the bagel halves.
Serve sprinkled with chopped fresh mint and lemon
zest and garnish with a few sprigs of fresh mint and
some salad leaves.

SPROUTING BAGEL

★ ★ ★ ★ ★

One for the health-conscious, this bagel is filled with low-fat cheese and sprouts.

SERVES 2

1 onion bagel

¼ cup low-fat cream cheese

¼ cup alfalfa sprouts

¼ cup bean sprouts

½ cup quartered cherry tomatoes

2 tbsp French dressing

salt and freshly ground black pepper

METHOD

Cut the bagel in half horizontally and toast. Divide the cream cheese between the bagel halves and spread evenly.

Place the alfalfa and bean sprouts in a bowl with the cherry tomato quarters. Toss to combine.

Divide the sprout mixture between the bagel halves. Sprinkle over the French dressing and season with salt and freshly ground black pepper to taste.

SUNSET BOULEVARD

★ ★ ★ ★ ★

A deliciously light and tangy combination of beets and orange, with the crunch of pine nuts.

SERVES 2

1 sesame seed bagel

butter or margarine, for spreading

1 cup diced cooked beet

2 small sweet oranges, segmented

1 tbsp pine nuts

finely grated orange zest, fresh mint leaves and sprigs, to garnish

For the dressing

2 tbsp hazelnut oil

1 tbsp fresh orange juice

2 tsp white wine vinegar

salt and freshly ground black pepper

METHOD

Cut the bagel in half horizontally and butter the cut surfaces. Place the beet, orange segments, and pine nuts in a bowl.

To make the dressing, mix together the hazelnut oil, orange juice, and vinegar. Season with salt and freshly ground black pepper and pour over the beet mixture. Toss the salad gently.

Pile the beet and orange mixture onto the bagel halves. Scatter over a little orange zest and a few mint leaves. Serve garnished with extra sprigs of fresh mint.

Sunset Boulevard

VEGETARIAN FRIDAY NIGHT BAGEL

★ ★ ★ ★ ★

A vegetarian alternative to chopped liver. This unusual chestnut recipe is so delicious, it might even convert a few carnivores.

SERVES 4

1 tbsp olive oil

1 small onion, finely chopped

1 clove of garlic, crushed

1 lb can chestnuts

4–5 tbsp dry red wine

salt and freshly ground black pepper

2 sesame seed bagels

butter or margarine, for spreading

1 hard-boiled egg

2 tbsp chopped fresh parsley

fresh parsley sprigs, to garnish

METHOD

Heat the oil in a frying pan and add the onion and garlic. Cook for about 5 minutes, until the onion has softened. Add the chestnuts and wine, stir well and cook gently for about 10 minutes, stirring occasionally.

Transfer the chestnut mixture to a food processor or blender and puree until you have the desired texture. Season with salt and freshly ground black pepper, then cool.

Cut the bagels in half horizontally and butter the cut surfaces. Divide the paté between the bagel halves, smoothing it out evenly.

Separate the egg white from the yolk and press separately through a sieve or tea-strainer. Use the sieved egg white and yolk to make alternate lines across the paté. Sprinkle with chopped parsley and serve each half garnished with a parsley sprig.

VIVA ESPAÑA

★ ★ ★ ★ ★

*A small omelet is perfect for this recipe for one. Alternatively make
a larger omelet and serve cut into wedges.*

SERVES 1

2 tbsp butter

¼ small onion, finely chopped

1 small potato, peeled and diced

⅓ red bell pepper, seeded and diced

⅓ yellow bell pepper, seeded and diced

1 tbsp chopped fresh parsley

salt and freshly ground black pepper

2 eggs, beaten

1 poppy seed bagel

butter or margarine, for spreading

2 tsp finely grated Cheddar cheese

pickled chilies and fresh parsley sprig, to garnish

METHOD

Melt the butter in a small frying pan and add the onion, potato, bell peppers, and all but a pinch of the parsley. Cook gently for about 10 minutes, stirring frequently, until the potato is cooked and browned.

Season the vegetables with salt and freshly ground black pepper, then pour in the beaten eggs. Cook the omelet on one side and broil the other, until golden.

Meanwhile, cut the bagel in half horizontally and toast. Butter the cut surfaces and sandwich the omelet in between the two halves.

Sprinkle the lid of the bagel with the reserved pinch of chopped parsley and the grated cheese. Garnish with pickled chilies and a sprig of flat leaf parsley.

TZATZIKI BAGEL

★ ★ ★ ★ ★

Perfect for a hot summer's day, the tzatziki mixture can be made in advance and kept in the fridge. Use to fill the bagels just before serving.

SERVES 2

1 cup Greek yoghurt

½ cup cucumber, peeled and finely diced

3–4 cloves of garlic, crushed

3 tbsp chopped fresh mint

salt and freshly ground black pepper

1 onion bagel

fresh mint sprigs, to garnish

METHOD

Put the yoghurt in a mixing bowl and stir in the cucumber, garlic, and mint. Season with salt and freshly ground black pepper. Cover and chill for at least 1 hour.

Cut the bagel in half horizontally and toast. Divide the tzatziki between the bagel halves. Serve garnished with sprigs of fresh mint.

WILD WEST BAGEL

★ ★ ★ ★ ★

Any combination of mushrooms is suitable for this recipe. Just remember to cook the more delicate mushrooms last.

SERVES 2

¼ cup butter or margarine

2 cloves of garlic, crushed

2 tsp dried thyme

3 cups mixed mushrooms, washed and sliced if appropriate

1 bagel

salt and freshly ground black pepper

fresh thyme sprigs, to garnish

METHOD

Melt the butter in a frying pan and add the garlic and thyme. Cook for about 1 minute, then add the mushrooms. Saute the mushrooms, stirring frequently, for about 5 minutes, until slightly browned.

Meanwhile, cut the bagel in half horizontally and toast. Divide the mushroom mixture between the bagel halves and season with salt and freshly ground black pepper.

Garnish with sprigs of fresh thyme.

Wild West Bagel

VEGGIE BURGER BAGEL

★ ★ ★ ★ ★

*Liven up your favorite veggie burger and serve it on a toasted
sesame bagel, with all the trimmings, of course!*

SERVES 2

2 veggie burgers

2 sesame seed bagels

butter or margarine, for spreading

2 tbsp mayonnaise

1 tomato, sliced

2–3 tbsp ketchup

a few lettuce leaves

salad leaves and fresh herbs, to garnish

METHOD

Cook the veggie burgers according to the manufacturer's instructions.

Meanwhile, cut the bagels in half horizontally and lightly toast. Butter the cut surfaces and place the bagel bases on individual serving plates.

To assemble the burger bagels, place a dollop of mayonnaise on each base and spread out evenly. Top with a few slices of tomato, then a little ketchup, followed by the veggie burger.

Add a few lettuce leaves, a little more ketchup, if you like, then place the bagel top in position. Serve with a few extra salad leaves and fresh herbs, to garnish.

VEGETARIAN DREAM

★ ★ ★ ★ ★

Bean paté is available from most supermarkets and health food stores, but you can use your own favorite variety of spread or paté.

SERVES 2

2 poppy seed bagels

butter or margarine, for spreading

½ cup bean paté

½ large avocado, peeled and sliced

2–3 tbsp mayonnaise

7 oz can mixed beans in water, drained

2 tbsp French dressing

2 tsp tomato paste

salt and freshly ground black pepper

parsley sprigs, to garnish

METHOD

Cut the bagels horizontally into three layers and butter.

Divide the bean paté between the bottom layers, then top with the sliced avocado. Spoon some mayonnaise on top, then position the middle layers.

Put the mixed beans in a bowl. Whisk the French dressing together with the tomato paste, then pour over the beans.

Divide the bean mixture between the bagels, then season with salt and freshly ground black pepper. Position the bagel lids and serve garnished with sprigs of parsley.

SUPER SUPPER BAGEL

★ ★ ★ ★ ★

This lentil and nut filled bagel is a meal in itself. Serve with a crisp salad and a glass of chilled white wine for the perfect meal.

SERVES 2

1 large bagel

2 tbsp olive oil

1 clove of garlic, crushed

2 tsp dried thyme

2 cups chopped mushrooms

½ cup drained cooked green lentils

¼ cup chopped cashew nuts, toasted

¼ cup wholewheat flour

¾ cup milk

1 cup grated sharp Cheddar cheese

salt and freshly ground black pepper

fresh thyme sprigs, to garnish

METHOD

Cut the bagel in half horizontally and remove the inner dough to make a hollow. Place the hollowed bagel halves in a shallow ovenproof dish.

Heat the oil in a frying pan and add the garlic and thyme. Cook for about 1 minute, then add the mushrooms. Cook for about 5 minutes, then stir in the lentils and cashew nuts. Continue to cook for 2–3 minutes.

Sprinkle over the flour and stir in well. Gradually pour in the milk, stirring continuously, until blended. Bring to a boil, stirring. Stir in the cheese until melted and season with salt and freshly ground black pepper.

Spoon the mixture into the hollowed bagels and around the edges in the dish. Bake in a preheated oven at 375°F for about 15–20 minutes, until the filling is golden. Serve immediately, garnished with sprigs of fresh thyme.

EASTERN PROMISE

★ ★ ★ ★ ★

Based on the traditional Middle Eastern speciality, Tabbouleh, the bulgur wheat needs to soak for at least 20 minutes in boiling water.

SERVES 4

½ cup bulgur wheat, soaked and drained

few green onions, chopped

2 tomatoes, sliced into wedges

¼ cup quartered black olives

¼ cup chopped fresh mint

¼ cup extra virgin olive oil

1 tbsp freshly squeezed lemon juice

2 cloves of garlic, finely chopped

salt and freshly ground black pepper

2 bagels

butter or margarine, for spreading

finely grated zest of 1 lemon

fresh mint sprigs and tomato slices, to garnish

METHOD

Place the bulgur wheat in a bowl with the green onions, tomatoes, olives, and mint. Drizzle over the olive oil and lemon juice, then stir in the chopped garlic. Season with salt and freshly ground black pepper. Mix well.

Cut the bagels in half horizontally and toast. Butter the cut surfaces and place on individual serving plates.

Top each bagel half generously with the bulgur mixture, then sprinkle over a little lemon zest. Serve garnished with sprigs of fresh mint and tomato slices.

Eastern Promise

THE BIG CHEESE

★ ★ ★ ★ ★

*Crisp on the outside with soft, warm, melted cheese on the inside,
this lightly toasted bagel is served with the sharp, sweet contrast of
gooseberry sauce. Or try raspberries for a change.*

SERVES 2

2 whole individual Camembert cheeses

1 egg, beaten

1 cup fine breadcrumbs

1 bagel

butter or margarine, for spreading

2 tbsp gooseberry jam

½ cup gooseberries in syrup, from a jar

fresh parsley sprigs, to garnish

METHOD

Coat the Camembert cheeses in the beaten egg, then
in the breadcrumbs. Place on a baking sheet and bake
in a preheated oven at 350°F for about 10–15
minutes, or until the cheese is warmed and melting.

Meanwhile, cut the bagel in half horizontally and
toast. Butter the cut surfaces.

Warm the gooseberry jam in a small saucepan and
add the gooseberries with about 3 tbsp syrup.

Serve a Camembert cheese on each bagel half,
with the gooseberry sauce as an accompaniment.
Garnish with sprigs of fresh parsley.

BAGEL SKINS

★ ★ ★ ★ ★

*Crispy and crunchy, naughty but nice – choose your favorite filling
to suit your taste.*

SERVES 2

2 bagels

vegetable oil, for deep frying

1 cup guacamole

1 cup grated Cheddar cheese

pinch of paprika

fresh parsley sprigs, to garnish

METHOD

Cut the bagels in half vertically and pull out the dough from the middle, making a hollow crescent.

Heat the oil to 325°F for deep frying. Fry the bagel crescents for about 5 minutes, until crisp and golden. Drain on absorbent paper towel.

Fill each crescent with guacamole, then top with grated cheese and paprika. Place on a baking sheet and broil for about 1 minute to melt the cheese. Serve immediately, garnished with sprigs of fresh parsley.

MEATLESS MAGIC

★ ★ ★ ★ ★

This is a tempting vegetarian bagel which even meat eaters will love.

SERVES 2

sunflower oil, for shallow frying

½ cup thinly sliced marinated tofu

1 clove of garlic, crushed

1 tbsp curry paste

½ cup baby corn

½ cup Chinese pea pods

¼ red bell pepper, seeded and cut into thin strips

½ cup vegetable stock

¼ cup dessicated coconut

3 tbsp chopped fresh coriander

1 bagel

fresh coriander sprigs, to garnish

METHOD

Heat the oil for shallow frying and fry the tofu strips for about 3–5 minutes, turning them over, until crisp and golden. Drain on absorbent paper towel.

Carefully transfer about 2 tbsp of the cooking oil to another frying pan and cook the garlic for about 1 minute. Stir in the curry paste and cook for a further minute.

Add the vegetables and cook for about 5 minutes, stirring frequently. Add the stock and coconut and cook gently for about 5 minutes, until the vegetables are just tender and the sauce has thickened.

Stir in the tofu strips and fresh coriander for the last minute of the cooking time.

Meanwhile, cut the bagel in half horizontally and lightly toast. Place the bagel halves on individual serving plates and top with the creamy tofu and vegetable mixture. Serve immediately, garnished with sprigs of fresh coriander.

ROCK 'N' ROLL BAGEL

★ ★ ★ ★ ★

A rich combination of leeks, mushrooms, and tomatoes with blue cheese.

SERVES 2

2 tbsp olive oil

1 clove of garlic, crushed

1 tbsp chopped fresh rosemary

½ leek, thinly sliced

1 cup quartered mushrooms

½ cup quartered cherry tomatoes

¼ cup crumbled blue cheese

2 bagels

butter or margarine, for spreading

fresh rosemary sprigs, to garnish

METHOD

Heat the oil in a frying pan and add the garlic and chopped rosemary. Cook for about 1 minute.

Add the leek and mushrooms and continue to cook for about 5 minutes, or until the vegetables are lightly browned. Add the cherry tomatoes and blue cheese and cook for a further minute.

Meanwhile, cut the bagels in half horizontally and toast. Butter the cut surfaces. Serve on individual plates with the blue cheese filling. Garnish with sprigs of fresh rosemary.

Rock 'n' Roll Bagel

SUMMER BREEZE

★ ★ ★ ★ ★

Tender cooked vegetable filling, coated in a light dressing and tossed together with sunflower seeds and freshly grated Parmesan cheese, all served on a lightly toasted bagel.

SERVES 2

1 cup fresh asparagus tips, trimmed

1 carrot, peeled and thinly sliced

2 tbsp hazelnut oil

1 tbsp sunflower oil

1 tbsp white wine vinegar

2 tsp fresh orange juice

salt and freshly ground black pepper

2 tbsp toasted sunflower seeds

1 sesame seed bagel

butter or margarine, for spreading

¼ cup freshly grated Parmesan cheese

fresh herb sprigs, to garnish

METHOD

Place the asparagus and sliced carrot in a steamer or small amount of water and cook for about 5 minutes, until just tender. Drain, if necessary. Place the vegetables in a bowl.

Mix together the hazelnut and sunflower oils, vinegar, and orange juice. Pour over the vegetables and toss to coat. Season with salt and freshly ground black pepper, then stir in the sunflower seeds.

Cut the bagel in half horizontally and lightly toast. Butter the cut surfaces and place on individual serving plates.

Arrange the vegetable mixture on top of each bagel half, then spoon over any remaining dressing. Sprinkle with Parmesan cheese and serve garnished with sprigs of fresh herbs.

HOMETY BAGEL

★ ★ ★ ★ ★

A warm, filling bagel, perfect served with lightly cooked carrots for a special supper-time treat.

SERVES 2

2 bagels

2 large potatoes, peeled and cut into pieces

¾ cup cauliflower florets

¼ cup butter or margarine

salt and freshly ground black pepper

¾ cup grated sharp Cheddar cheese

2 tsp chopped fresh parsley, to garnish

METHOD

Cut a thin slice horizontally off the top of the bagel. Pull out the dough from the inside of the bagel to make a hollow ring.

Simmer the potatoes and cauliflower separately in boiling water, until the potatoes are cooked and the cauliflower is just tender. Drain.

Mash the potatoes with the butter, salt and freshly ground black pepper and ½ cup of the grated cheese. Carefully stir in the cauliflower florets, without breaking them.

Pile the potato mixture into each bagel, then top with the reserved grated cheese.

Place the bagels on a baking sheet and cook in a preheated oven at 400°F for about 15–20 minutes, until the filling is golden and the bagel is crisp. Serve garnished with chopped parsley.

SQUASHED BAGEL

★ ★ ★ ★ ★

*Any combination of squashes works well for this recipe. Remember
the more colorful, the more attractive the finished result will be.*

SERVES 4

1 lb mixed squashes, such as pumpkin, acorn, prince
etc., peeled and diced

¼ cup butter

2 cloves of garlic, crushed

squeeze of fresh lemon juice

3 tbsp chopped fresh dill

4 bagels

butter or margarine, for spreading

½ cup grated Cheddar cheese

salt and freshly ground black pepper

fresh dill sprigs, to garnish

METHOD

Cook the diced squashes in boiling water or steam for
about 5 minutes, or until just tender. Drain well.

Melt the butter in a frying pan and saute the garlic
for about 1 minute. Add the cooked squashes, with
the lemon juice and chopped dill. Cook for about 3–5
minutes.

Meanwhile, cut the bagels in half horizontally and
toast. Butter the bases, then place them on individual
serving plates.

Arrange the bagel tops on a baking sheet and
sprinkle over the grated cheese. Broil until melted.

Divide the squash mixture between the bagel bases
and season with salt and freshly ground black pepper.
Top each one with a cheese covered lid and garnish
with a sprig of fresh dill.

RATABAGEL

★ ★ ★ ★ ★

*This traditional mixture of vegetables, cooked in a rich garlicky
tomato sauce, is perfect served with a toasted bagel to mop up the
delicious sauce.*

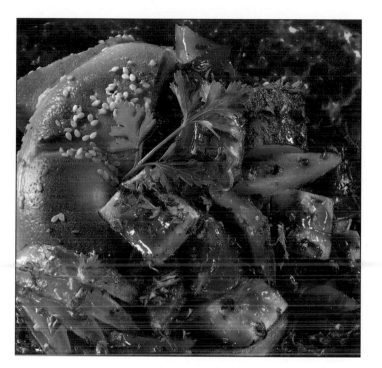

SERVES 2

3 tbsp olive oil

2 cloves of garlic, crushed

½ onion, sliced

½ red bell pepper, seeded and cut into pieces

½ yellow bell pepper, seeded and cut into pieces

1 zucchini, cut into pieces

1 tomato, cut into wedges

3–4 tbsp chopped fresh parsley

½ cup vegetable stock

3 tbsp tomato paste

salt and freshly ground black pepper

1 sesame seed bagel

fresh parsley sprigs, to garnish

METHOD

Heat the oil in a large frying pan and add the garlic
and onion. Fry for about 3 minutes, until the onion has
browned. Add the bell peppers and zucchini and
continue to cook for a further 5 minutes.

Add the tomato, chopped parsley, stock, and
tomato paste and season with salt and freshly ground
black pepper. Cover and cook gently for about 10–15
minutes, stirring frequently.

Cut the bagel in half horizontally and toast. Cut
each half into two equal portions and serve with the
ratatouille mixture. Garnish with a sprig of fresh
parsley.

SWEET
BAGELS

★ ★ ★ ★ ★

BREAD 'N' BUTTER BAGEL

★ ★ ★ ★ ★

Serve this warm and filling pudding bagel with whipped cream or custard.

SERVES 2

2 cinnamon and raisin bagels

1 egg, beaten

finely grated zest of ½ lemon

¼ cup superfine sugar

2 tbsp raisins

pinch of grated nutmeg

1 tbsp melted butter

3 tbsp milk

METHOD

Cut a thin slice off the top of each bagel and scoop out the dough from the middle with your fingers, making a hollow ring. Place the scooped-out dough in a mixing bowl and put the hollowed out bagels in a shallow ovenproof dish.

Add the beaten egg to the bagel dough in the mixing bowl, with the lemon zest, sugar, raisins, nutmeg, melted butter, and milk. Mix well.

Spoon the egg mixture into the hollowed bagels. Bake in a preheated oven at 375°F for about 25–30 minutes, or until the mixture is golden. Serve immediately.

ORANGE LOCKSHEN PUDDING BAGEL

★ ★ ★ ★ ★

Based on the Jewish theme, this bagel uses a little creative licence, resulting in a real bagel speciality.

SERVES 2

2 cinnamon and raisin bagels

2 tbsp melted butter or margarine

1 egg

¼ cup superfine sugar

pinch of ground cinnamon

finely grated zest of ½ orange

few drops of orange extract

2 tbsp golden raisins

½ cup vermicelli pasta, broken into small pieces, cooked in boiling water and drained

sifted confectioners' sugar, to decorate

METHOD

Cut a thin slice off the top of each bagel and scoop out the dough from the middle with your fingers, to make a hollow ring. Discard the dough and top. Place the hollowed bagels in a shallow ovenproof dish.

Using a pastry brush, coat the inside of each hollowed bagel with a little of the melted butter.

Place the egg and sugar in a mixing bowl and whisk, using an electric hand mixer, until frothy. Whisk in the cinnamon, orange zest, and extract. Add the golden raisins and cooked vermicelli to the whisked mixture and stir to coat evenly.

Spoon the vermicelli mixture into the hollowed bagels. Bake in a preheated oven at 375°F for about 25–30 minutes, or until the mixture is set and golden. Serve warm, dusted generously with sifted confectioners' sugar.

BANANA BAGEL SPLIT

A rich banana and cream topped bagel – ideal for adults and children alike.

SERVES 2

1 cinnamon and raisin bagel

1 cup heavy cream

3 tbsp sifted confectioners' sugar

few drops of banana flavoring

2 bananas, peeled and cut in half lengthways

2–3 tbsp maple syrup

colored sprinkles, to decorate

METHOD

Cut the bagel in half horizontally and toast. Keep warm.

Put the cream in a bowl with the confectioners' sugar and banana flavoring. Whisk, using an electric hand mixer, until it forms soft peaks.

Place the bagel halves on individual serving plates and divide about two-thirds of the cream mixture between them.

Lay the split bananas on top of the cream, then top with the remaining cream mixture. Drizzle with maple syrup, then cover with sprinkles, to decorate.

PEANUT CHOCCA BAGEL

★ ★ ★ ★ ★

A perfect after-school snack for kids.

SERVES 2

2 cinnamon and raisin bagels

butter or margarine, for spreading

4–5 tbsp crunchy peanut butter

3–4 tbsp chocolate spread

2 tbsp sifted chocolate drink powder, to decorate

METHOD

Cut each bagel horizontally to make three even layers and butter.

Divide the peanut butter between the two bagel bases and spread evenly. Place the middle bagel layer on top of the peanut butter and smooth over the chocolate spread.

Top with the bagel lid and serve dusted with sifted chocolate drink powder.

CHOCOLATE DREAM

★ ★ ★ ★ ★

This bagel is a must for chocaholics.

SERVES 2

1 cinnamon and raisin bagel

4 scoops of chocolate ice-cream

4–5 tbsp chocolate sauce

2–3 tbsp grated chocolate, to decorate

METHOD

Cut the bagel in half horizontally and toast. Place each half on an individual serving plate.

Place two scoops of chocolate ice-cream on each bagel half, while the bagel is still warm.

Drizzle over the chocolate sauce and serve immediately, sprinkled with grated chocolate.

Chocolate Dream

BAGELOVA

★ ★ ★ ★ ★

*Based on the traditional Pavlova idea, this bagel is quick and simple
to prepare and tastes delicious.*

SERVES 2

1 cinnamon and raisin bagel

½ cup heavy cream

2 tbsp sifted confectioners' sugar, plus extra for dusting

few drops of vanilla extract

2 cups mixed soft fruits, such as blueberries, raspberries,
chopped strawberries, and kiwi-fruit

fresh mint sprigs, to decorate

METHOD

Cut the bagel in half horizontally and place on individual serving plates.

Put the cream in a mixing bowl and add the confectioners' sugar and vanilla extract. Whisk with an electric hand mixer until it forms soft peaks.

Divide the cream mixture between the bagel halves, then pile the mixed fruit on top. Dust generously with sifted confectioners' sugar and serve immediately, decorated with sprigs of fresh mint.

BAGEL HÉLÈNE

★ ★ ★ ★ ★

*A traditional dessert duo of pears and chocolate sauce, served on
a sweet soft bagel, topped with whipped cream.*

SERVES 2

1 cinnamon and raisin bagel

½ cup heavy cream

1 tbsp sifted confectioners' sugar

few drops of vanilla extract

4 canned pear halves in syrup, drained

4–5 tbsp chocolate sauce

tiny lemon geranium or fresh mint sprigs, to decorate

METHOD

Cut the bagel in half horizontally and place on individual serving plates.

Put the cream in a mixing bowl and add the confectioners' sugar and vanilla extract. Whisk, using an electric hand mixer, until it forms soft peaks.

Divide the cream mixture between the bagel bases and spread out evenly. Top with the pear halves, then drizzle generously with chocolate sauce. Decorate with tiny sprigs of lemon geranium or mint. Serve immediately.

SUNSHINE BAGEL

★ ★ ★ ★ ★

An elegant and original dinner party dessert to stun your guests.

SERVES 4

2 cinnamon and raisin bagels

2 cups heavy cream

¼ cup sifted confectioners' sugar

few drops of vanilla extract

1 tbsp orange liqueur

4 small caramelized oranges in syrup, drained (reserving ¾ cup syrup) and sliced

1½ tbsp arrowroot

finely grated orange zest and fresh mint sprigs, to decorate

METHOD

Cut the bagels in half horizontally and place on individual serving plates.

Put the cream in a mixing bowl and add the confectioners' sugar, vanilla extract, and orange liqueur. Whisk with an electric hand mixer until it forms soft peaks.

Use the cream mixture to fill a piping bag fitted with a medium star nozzle. Pipe decoratively on top of each bagel half.

Arrange the sliced oranges on top of the cream, then finish piping decoratively on top.

Mix enough of the reserved orange syrup with the arrowroot to make a smooth paste. Heat the remaining syrup in a small saucepan, until boiling. Stir in the arrowroot paste and return to the boil, stirring continuously, until thickened, shiny, and smooth. Cool slightly.

Drizzle the orange sauce over the bagel halves. Decorate with orange zest and sprigs of fresh mint.

THE BIG APPLE
★ ★ ★ ★ ★

The way to eat this fruity extravaganza is warm with a generous helping of whipped cream.

SERVES 2

2 dessert apples, peeled and chopped

2 tbsp caster sugar

pinch of ground cinnamon

1 tbsp butter or margarine, plus extra for spreading

1 cinnamon and raisin bagel

whipped cream, to serve

METHOD

Place the chopped apple, sugar, ground cinnamon, and butter in a saucepan with 4–5 tbsp water. Bring the apple mixture to the boil, then simmer for about 5 minutes, until the apple is tender. Drain and cool until warm.

Meanwhile, cut the bagel in half horizontally and pull out the bagel dough from the middle of each half to make a hollow ring.

Butter the inside of the bagel rings, then place in a very low oven to warm through.

Spoon the apple mixture into the warmed, hollowed out bagels and serve with a dollop of whipped cream.

BLACK FOREST BAGEL
★ ★ ★ ★ ★

A luxurious combination of black cherries and cream coated in a velvety smooth, cherry sauce.

SERVES 2

2 cinnamon and raisin bagels

¼ cup kirsch liqueur

14 oz can black cherries in syrup, drained, syrup reserved

1 cup heavy cream

2 tbsp sifted confectioners' sugar

few drops of vanilla extract

1 tbsp arrowroot

fresh mint sprigs, to decorate

METHOD

Slice a thin layer off the top of each bagel, then hollow it out with your fingers, pulling out the dough from the center of the bagel.

Sprinkle about 1 tbsp of the kirsch over the insides of each bagel. Place all but a few of the cherries in the hollowed bagels.

Put the cream in a mixing bowl and add the confectioners' sugar and vanilla extract. Whisk, using an electric hand mixer, until the cream forms soft peaks. Divide the cream mixture between the bagels, piling it up high.

Put about ½ cup of the reserved cherry syrup in a small saucepan. In a small bowl, mix the arrowroot with enough of the cherry syrup to make a smooth paste. Heat the syrup until boiling. Stir in the arrowroot mixture and return to the boil, stirring continuously, until shiny and thickened. Cool slightly.

Arrange the reserved cherries on the cream on each bagel, then pour over the warm sauce and serve immediately, decorated with sprigs of fresh mint.

Black Forest Bagel

A TRIFLE BAGEL

★ ★ ★ ★ ★

*A perfect treat for a special Sunday lunch for all the family.
Multiply the quantities of ingredients, depending on how many Trifle
Bagels you'll need.*

SERVES 2

1 cinnamon and raisin bagel

7 oz can raspberries in syrup, drained

6–7 tbsp prepared vanilla pudding

½ cup heavy cream

colored sprinkles, to decorate

METHOD

Cut the bagel in half horizontally and scoop out the dough from the middle, using your fingers, to make a hollow ring.

Put the bagel halves on individual serving plates and divide all but a few of the raspberries between them. Reserve the remainder. Press the raspberries down gently in the bagel bases, then spoon the pudding on top.

Put the cream in a mixing bowl and whisk with an electric hand mixer until it forms soft peaks. Divide the cream between the bagels, then scatter over the reserved raspberries. Cover with sprinkles, then serve immediately.

TROPICAL DREAM

★ ★ ★ ★ ★

*This bagel is colorful and fruity. You can use whatever tropical fruits
you can find and mix them with other tiny soft fruits.*

SERVES 2

1 cinnamon and raisin bagel

½ cup heavy cream

1 tbsp confectioners' sugar

few drops of vanilla extract

1 cup mixed tropical fruits, such as star fruit, papaya, kiwi-fruit, and other soft fruits

5–6 tbsp tropical fruit juice

2 tbsp arrowroot

tiny lemon geranium sprigs, to decorate

METHOD

Cut the bagel in half horizontally and toast. Place each bagel half on an individual serving plate.

Put the cream in a mixing bowl with the confectioners' sugar and vanilla extract. Whisk with an electric hand mixer until it forms soft peaks.

Divide the cream mixture between the bagel halves and spread out evenly. Arrange the fruits on top.

Mix enough of the tropical fruit juice with the arrowroot in a small bowl to make a smooth paste. Heat the remaining juice in a saucepan until boiling. Stir in the arrowroot paste and bring the sauce back to the boil, stirring continuously, until thickened, smooth, and shiny. Cool slightly.

Drizzle the sauce over the bagel halves. Decorate with tiny sprigs of lemon geranium, to serve.

Tropical Dream

PECAN TOPPERS

★ ★ ★ ★ ★

These nutty bagels are deliciously sweet and sticky.

SERVES 2

1 cinnamon and raisin bagel

butter or margarine, for spreading

4–5 tbsp butterscotch sauce

1 cup chopped pecan nuts

METHOD

Cut the bagel in half horizontally and butter the cut surfaces. Lightly toast, until golden.

Place the butterscotch sauce in a bowl and stir in the chopped pecan nuts. Divide the pecan mixture between the bagels and spread evenly. Serve immediately.

STRAWBERRY FAYRE

★ ★ ★ ★ ★

This delightful summertime extravaganza combines ice-cream with whipped cream, sweet strawberries, and a freshly baked, warm cinnamon bagel.

SERVES 2

2 cinnamon and raisin bagels

½ cup heavy cream

2 tbsp sifted powdered sugar

few drops of vanilla extract

1 cup sliced fresh strawberries

2 large scoops of luxury strawberry ice-cream

2–3 tbsp strawberry sauce

strawberries, sifted confectioners' sugar, and fresh mint sprigs, to decorate

METHOD

Cut a 'V' shape out of the center of each bagel. Discard the 'V' shape, slice the bagels in half, and place the bagel bases in a low oven to warm.

Meanwhile, put the cream in a mixing bowl with the powdered sugar and vanilla extract. Whisk, using an electric hand mixer, until the cream forms soft peaks.

Place the bagel bases on individual serving plates and divide the whipped cream mixture between them. Arrange the sliced strawberries on top.

Put a scoop of ice-cream on top of the strawberries, then drizzle with strawberry sauce. Decorate with a strawberry, sifted confectioners' sugar and sprigs of fresh mint.

INDEX

★ ★ ★ ★ ★